Disney · PIXA...

EXPLORE MEXICO

A *Coco* Discovery Book

W9-CKZ-641

Lars Ortiz

In Association with
Marcela Davison Avilés, Cultural Consultant

Lerner Publications • Minneapolis

Dedicated to Elodie and my whole family —L.O.

For my parents —M.D.A.

Cultural consultation and additional content provided by
Marcela Davison Avilés

Lerner Publications Company
An imprint of Lerner Publishing Group, Inc.
241 First Avenue North
Minneapolis, MN 55401 USA

For reading levels and more information, look up this title at
www.lernerbooks.com.

Main body text set in Mikado.
Typeface provided by HVD Fonts.

Library of Congress Cataloging-in-Publication Data

Names: Ortiz, Lars, 1984– author.
Title: Explore Mexico : a Coco discovery book / Lars Ortiz
  ; in association with Marcela Davison Avilés, cultural
  consultant.
Description: Minneapolis : Lerner Publications, [2020] | Series:
  Disney learning discovery books | Includes bibliographical
  references and index. | Audience: Grades 4-6. | Audience:
  Ages 7–11.
Identifiers: LCCN 2019005156 (print) | LCCN 2019005665
  (ebook) | ISBN 9781541578296 (eb pdf) | ISBN 9781541578272
  (lb : alk. paper) | ISBN 9781541578289 (pb : alk. paper)
Subjects: LCSH: Mexico—Juvenile literature. | Mexico—
  Civilization—Juvenile literature.
Classification: LCC F1208.5 (ebook) | LCC F1208.5 .O788 2019
  (print) | DDC 972—dc23

LC record available at https://lccn.loc.gov/2019005156

Manufactured in the United States of America
1-46933-47811-5/17/2019

CONTENTS

WELCOME TO MEXICO!

¡Bienvenidos! **Let's explore the beautiful land of diverse communities, languages, and traditions that Miguel and his family call home.**

Where in the World?

Mexico is located on the continent of North America. The country borders both land and sea. The Pacific Ocean lies to the west and the Gulf of Mexico to the east. The countries of Guatemala and Belize are to the south. The United States is to Mexico's north.

Mexico

Meet the People

The people who live in Mexico have many origins. Some are **indigenous** to the land, such as **Aztec** and **Maya** people. Other Mexicans are **descendants** from people in European countries, including Spain, France, Germany, and Austria. Many Mexicans also have African or Asian roots. The word *mestizo* is used in **Latin America** to describe people of blended heritage. The people of Mexico represent a combination of many different backgrounds.

Mexico at a Glance

Mexico has thirty-one states and about 132 million people. Mexico City, the nation's capital, has almost 9 million **residents**. The Mexican flag is green, white, and red. Its central image shows an eagle eating a snake while landing on the nopal cactus.

LAND AND CLIMATE

Miguel's homeland has a wide variety of climates, **biomes**, and geographical features. Let's learn more about them together!

On the Ring of Fire

Geologists call the massive area along the edges of the Pacific Ocean the Ring of Fire. Here, tectonic plates, or huge pieces of Earth's crust, rub against one another. The movement can trigger **tremors**, major earthquakes, and volcanic eruptions. Mexico, the US, and many other countries lie on the Ring of Fire. Technologies such as earthquake detectors and quake-resistant building materials can lessen the impact of geologic events.

Mountains and Volcanoes

Popocatépetl

Mountain ranges stretch through most of Mexico. Popocatépetl (poh-poh-kah-TEH-peh-tuhl) and Iztaccíhuatl (ee-stahk-SEE-wah-tuhl) are two famous active volcanoes located outside Mexico City. In the **Nahuatl** (nah-WAH-tuhl) language, Popocatépetl means "smoking mountain" and Iztaccíhuatl means "white lady." Some Mexicans call the volcanoes El Popo and Izta for short.

From Deserts to Tropical Forests

Mexico is so vast that the **climate** varies depending on where you are, creating many interesting biomes. You can explore dry deserts in the north and temperate forests in the central and southern parts of the country. In the south and southeast of Mexico, you'll find tropical rain forests!

Coasts and Beaches

Mexico has 5,800 miles (9,330 km) of ocean coastline and some of the most beautiful beaches in the world. Mexicans and visitors from around the world flock to the beaches all year. Cancun, Los Cabos, Playa del Carmen, and Acapulco are home to many popular beaches. Come and explore them for yourself, but make sure to bring some sunscreen!

PLANTS AND ANIMALS

Miguel has many friends, and one of his best friends is a dog! Dante accompanies Miguel on his adventures. Mexico has many interesting animals and plants. Some, including dogs like Dante, are common. Other animals, such as the jaguar, are in danger of becoming **extinct**.

Xoloitzcuintli

The Xoloitzcuintli (shoh-loh-its-KWINT-lee) is a mostly hairless breed of dog. These dogs make excellent pets. Just like Dante! Xolo dogs have been present in Mexico for thousands of years. They were sacred guides and companions of the Aztecs in daily life. Xolos also played important roles in Aztec mythology about the afterlife.

More Mammals

jaguar

Hundreds of mammals live in Mexico, including monkeys, anteaters, and **jaguars**. Some indigenous people revered jaguars and believed they had godlike abilities of power and courage. But modern jaguars are in danger. They are threatened by **habitat** loss and illegal hunting. The Mexican government and groups such as the Northern Jaguar Project preserve land where the cats can live in peace.

Birds

More than one thousand bird **species** call Mexico home. The quetzal has bright colors and long, flowing tail feathers. Indigenous people have long **revered** the bird's feathers, which they use in ceremonies and for costumes. Quetzals live in wet climates and eat fruits and insects.

Plants

Mexico is home to countless species of plants. Brightly colored flowers such as the jacaranda are common. If you come to Mexico City when the jacaranda are in bloom, you'll see the streets lined in bright purple! Fruit trees that grow delicious mangoes and avocados dot the landscape, and farmers grow cacao trees to make chocolate. People use plants to make food, medicine, **dye**, and many other goods.

jacaranda

9

DIVERSE PEOPLE

Miguel and his family observe many traditions. People take part in many different cultural celebrations in Mexico. Mexico's population includes communities from different backgrounds and cultures. Let's meet some of them!

Mesoamerica

Scholars refer to the historical and cultural region formed by Mexico and Central America as Mesoamerica. Many groups, tribes, and kingdoms created important **civilizations** in this region. Five major civilizations formed the foundation of modern Mexico. These include the **Olmec**, the Teotihuacán (tee-oh-tee-wah-KAHN), the Toltec, the Aztec, and the Maya.

Aztecs

The Aztec civilization flourished from 1300 to 1521. The food, clothing, and other traditions of the Aztecs still have a central influence on Mexican culture. The Aztecs were highly skilled engineers who built bridges, **aqueducts**, and artificial islands called chinampas. The Aztecs developed formal education and training for much of its population. Nahuatl, the Aztec language, is spoken widely throughout the country.

chinampas

Maya

The history of the Maya people in Mexico goes back thousands of years. Ancient Maya made incredible advances in mathematics, **astronomy**, and **architecture**. They were one of the civilizations to develop the concept of zero. They also discovered that Earth takes about 365 days to go around the sun. The Maya built complex cities and created beautiful works of art. Today, the Maya people thrive in Mexico and are an essential part of the country's culture.

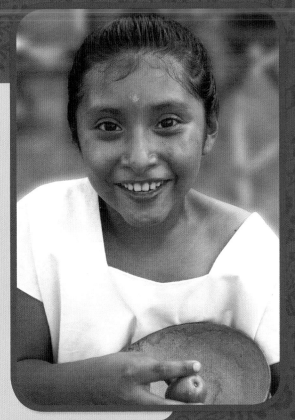

Mestizo

In Mexico, *mestizo* is a term that usually refers to people who consider themselves of a blended cultural heritage. For example, they may have both indigenous and European ancestors. Many Mexicans consider themselves mestizo. Other Mexicans identify as members of an indigenous people or immigrants from other countries.

LANGUAGES

Miguel and his family speak Spanish, but many different languages are spoken in Mexico. The country has sixty-eight national languages! Let's learn more about the languages people speak in Mexico.

Indigenous Languages

Sixty-three of Mexico's national languages are indigenous. Nahuatl is spoken by more than a million modern Mexicans. Many of our common words derive from Nahuatl, including avocado, chocolate, and coyote. Yucatec Maya, Mixtec, and Zapotec are just a few of the other indigenous languages spoken in Mexico. Speakers of Mixtec might call themselves Ñuudzahui (nyoo-DZAH-wee), which means "People of the Rain."

A sixteenth-century Aztec manuscript

Spanish

More than 90 percent of Mexicans speak Spanish. Did you know that nouns are either **masculine** or **feminine** in Spanish? *El libro* is a masculine noun that means "the book." *La mesa* is feminine and means "the table." Most nouns that end in an *o* are masculine, and those that end in *a* are usually feminine.

Trilling and Other Sounds

Spanish words with double *r*'s, such as *perro*, the word for "dog," have a special sound. Speakers must roll, or trill, the letters. Rolling *r*'s sound a bit like a small motor. Can you roll your *r*'s? Try it! The squiggly line above the letter *n* in some Spanish words is a tilde. The ñ combines the *n* sound and the *y* sound. For example, *año*, the Spanish word for year, sounds like AH-nyoh. If a word has a double *l*, it is pronounced like a *y*. *Llorar*, which means "to cry," sounds like yohr-AHR.

PLACES TO LIVE

Miguel and his family live in the town of Santa Cecilia. Santa Cecilia is also the name for the **patron saint** of music. Mexico is filled with many cities, towns, and villages that resemble Miguel's hometown.

Oaxaca

Oaxaca is both a state and a city in southern Mexico. The towns and villages in this region are the inspiration for Miguel's hometown. Oaxaca is famous for its beautiful buildings, **folk** art, dance, and music.

Towns

Many residents live in smaller towns, or pueblos. Pueblos often have beautiful town squares and detailed churches. With music, art, and celebrations, there's plenty to do in a pueblo. Some people who live in pueblos may travel to a big city for work.

Cities

Mexico City is the largest city in Mexico. The majority of Mexico's population lives in a large city. These **urban** areas feature busy streets, exciting music and art scenes, universities, and modern businesses.

Countryside

The Mexican countryside features many ranchos, or small, family-owned ranches. Farmers grow fruits and vegetables, and ranchers raise **livestock**.

FAMILY LIFE

Miguel's family members—the living ones and those in the Land of the Dead—are an important part of his life. Miguel is raised by his extended family. That's a lot of hugs, kisses, and pinched cheeks!

The Importance of Family

Miguel and many of his relatives live together as an extended family. Miguel lives with his parents, aunts, uncles, cousins, grandparents, and great-grandmother, Mamá Coco. People in Mexico have diverse family traditions and living arrangements. The importance of family remains a central part of the culture.

What's in a Name?

Names in Mexico often include a person's first name, middle name, father's last name, and mother's last name. It might also include a married name. Many people have full names that combine Spanish and indigenous names. Including these names is one way to recognize a person's heritage and family ties.

Respecting Your Elders

Mexican people honor their elders in many ways. They may show older people respect by using *usted*, the formal word for "you," to refer to them. Sometimes the best way to respect your elders is by listening to their insights and stories, as Miguel and his family learned. After all, Mamá Coco had an important history to share!

DÍA DE MUERTOS

Coco takes place during Día de Muertos, or Day of the Dead. Millions of people in Mexico and other countries take part in the holiday each year.

Holiday Tradition

Día de Muertos begins on October 31 and lasts through November 2. The important celebration has its roots in Aztec tradition and is one of the most deeply revered customs in Mexico. The holiday honors ancestors and loved ones who have passed away.

Remember Me

Also called Día de los Muertos in some regions of Mexico, the holiday is a time to remember. Families join together to make a memory about loved ones who have died, such as the relatives Miguel meets on his journey. During this holiday, people remember loved ones through family **rituals**. These include creating a table with art, flowers, and **mementos** of loved ones, visiting a cemetery, and eating a meal together.

Walk Together

In some communities, Mexicans organize a traditional **procession** to a cemetery during Día de Muertos. The people might play music as they walk, and kids may paint their faces like a calavera, or skull. Some kids even dress like a calaca, a skeleton.

THE OFRENDA

Miguel and his family honor their ancestors by creating an ofrenda in their home. This is a type of homemade altar that features remembrances of loved ones. Some believe that honoring ancestors with an ofrenda creates an invitation for their spirits to reunite with their families for a short time.

The Altar

Many families in Mexico create ofrendas in their homes or at cemeteries during Día de Muertos. An ofrenda consists of at least three levels. Some have as many as seven. The top level represents heaven. The middle of the ofrenda stands for Earth. The lower level is Mictlan, meaning the "Land of the Dead."

Ofrenda Decorations

People decorate ofrendas to create a visual remembrance of ancestors or loved ones who have died. Decorations might include pictures of ancestors or items that had meaning to dead loved ones. People also use **incense**, candles, and the orange petals of the *cempasúchil*, or marigold. They might put food, such as **pan de muerto**, drinks, and other objects on ofrendas. What a beautiful offering!

Deep Meaning

Each object on an ofrenda has a special meaning. Candles and marigold petals guide the spirits of loved ones to the altar. **Copal** incense is burned to purify the souls of the spirits. Pan de muerto and other favorite foods are offered as a way to honor loved ones.

OTHER FESTIVALS

Día de Muertos is one of the most famous Mexican holidays. However, people in Mexico have plenty of other reasons to celebrate. Festivals and holidays take place throughout the country at different times of the year. Let's learn about a few more holidays that Miguel and his family might celebrate!

Independence Day

Mexicans celebrate the country's independence from Spain on September 16. People throughout the country celebrate with music, parades, and fireworks. The *grito*, or cry for independence, is another part of the celebration. The passionate grito **commemorates** a priest named Miguel Hidalgo y Costilla, who made the call for independence in 1810.

Day of the Virgin of Guadalupe

On December 12, many Mexicans honor the Virgin Mary, who they also call the Virgin of Guadalupe. She is the patron saint of Mexico. Legend says she appeared to a man outside of Mexico City. She asked for a church to be built where she appeared. To many Mexicans, the Virgin of Guadalupe represents protection, hope, and acceptance.

Benito Juárez Day

On the third Monday in March, Mexicans celebrate former president Benito Juárez. A hero to many, Juárez is best known for making important national **reforms**, including helping poor people. He was Mexico's first president of indigenous origin.

¡FIESTA!

Miguel and his family love a fiesta. You might hear him let out a loud shout of joy. This shout is also called a grito, like the cry for independence. Fiestas are great times to gather with friends and family and meet new people. Here are just a few reasons to throw a fiesta in Mexico!

Birthdays

Mexicans may invite their friends over to eat some cake on their birthday. They might even sing "Las Mañanitas," the traditional Mexican birthday song. Some people hang a **piñata** from a high place, put on a blindfold, and spin around. Then they try to hit the piñata with a stick. If they break it open, they'll find candy or toys.

Weddings

Weddings celebrate a marriage between two people and bring families together from all parts of Mexico. These events are joyous occasions for the whole family. Get ready for music and dancing!

Quinceañera

The quinceañera, or quince, is a special celebration thrown on a girl's fifteenth birthday. The event marks her growth into womanhood. Common traditions include a religious service followed by a party with friends and family. The birthday girl usually wears a beautiful dress and special jewelry on this important day.

FOOD

Food plays an important part in bringing family and friends together. Families like Miguel's might relax and talk around the table for hours after a meal. This special time is called *sobremesa*. Let's find out more about Mexican food!

Basics of the Diet

Maize, another word for corn, provides a foundation for many delicious Mexican dishes. It can be grilled or made into casseroles. People use cornmeal to make tortillas, an important component of dishes such as enchiladas and tacos. Other common foods include avocados, peppers, tomatoes, plantains, and frijoles, or beans. The rich flavors of Mexican cuisine make it popular around the world.

Fruits and Vegetables

Mexico's climate makes it an ideal place for growing fruits. These include limes, oranges, pineapples, mangoes, **papayas**, coconuts, **guavas**, bananas, passion fruit, pomegranates, tomatoes, avocados, and more! Vegetable farmers grow nopals (prickly pear cactus), **chayote**, and **jicama**. **Tomatillos** and chili peppers add spice to cooking.

avocados

papayas

A Blending of Influences

Mexican food includes features from many different cultures and communities. Europeans brought rice from Asia to Mexico in the sixteenth century. It became a big part of Mexican cuisine. The modern tortilla has Spanish, Arabic, and indigenous origins. **Tamales** and **mole** sauce have indigenous roots. Can you name a food you enjoy that comes from a blending of different influences?

tamales

Let's Eat and Drink!

Agua de jamaica, or hibiscus tea, is a common Mexican drink that is sure to quench your thirst. Dinner might include pozole, a warm meat and vegetable soup. You might also try *chiles en nogada*, which are stuffed peppers covered in a walnut cream sauce. Leave room for dessert! You wouldn't want to miss the *pastel tres leches*, a cake made with three different types of milk.

MUSICAL HERITAGE

Miguel loves music and dreams of becoming a professional musician. Music has a special way of stirring emotions and bringing people together. Like many aspects of Mexican culture, the country's music reflects a wide variety of influences and origins.

Early Music

For hundreds of years, indigenous peoples have used instruments to create music. Early musicians made drums, rattles, whistles, trumpets, and flutes from wood or clay. Shells and other natural items were also used to create **percussion** instruments. One unique example is the *quijada*, made from the jawbone of a donkey. The Maya crafted a special instrument using a drum, a string, and sticks to mimic a jaguar's roar.

flutes

drum

rattle

Spanish Influences

Spanish people introduced many instruments to Mexico, such as guitars, harps, violins, and other stringed instruments. These instruments were later adopted for Mexican folk music. They are still popular in Mexican music today!

Mexican Baroque

During the **Baroque period** (about 1600 to 1750), Spanish chapel masters taught their musical style to native peoples. The Spanish hoped to convert the indigenous population to Christianity. Indigenous music makers began to mix their music with Spanish and other European musical styles. This blend of traditions and instruments created a new style called Mexican Baroque. It often combined European religious music with indigenous percussion instruments.

drum

BLENDING OF MUSICAL STYLES

Miguel can hear many musical styles in Mexico. These styles and many of the instruments associated with them began in different regions of the country. Mexican musical styles have indigenous, European, and African roots.

Son Jarocho

Son jarocho style began in the Veracruz region along Mexico's Gulf Coast. The music features indigenous, Caribbean, and African influences. Common son jarocho instruments include the jarana and the *requinto*. These guitarlike instruments make a high-pitched sound. The *arpa jarocha*, or harp, is another main feature of this style. Miguel and Hector sing "Un Poco Loco" in the son jarocho style.

Son Huasteco

The region in northeastern Mexico called La Huasteca gets its name from an indigenous group called the Huastec. That's where *son huasteco* began. This music is known for **falsetto** singing and skilled violin playing. Son huasteco bands are often a **trio**.

Son Jalisciense

Son jalisciense began in the west coast state of Jalisco. Son jalisciense uses the vihuela, a small guitar, and the *guitarrón*, a large bass guitar. Violins, standard guitars, trumpets, and harps may also take part. Mariachi is the most popular form of son jalisciense music. A mariachi band plays during Ernesto de la Cruz's performance of "Remember Me."

Banda

Banda bands started in the state of Sinaloa and can be found throughout Mexico. They often consist of brass, woodwind, and percussion instruments. Banda includes a wide variety of music types, including waltzes, polkas, **corridos**, and more. See if you can spot some of these instruments during the talent show scene in the Land of the Dead!

DANCE

Wherever there is music in Mexico, dancing is sure to follow. Mexican dance styles often feature colorful costumes, festive local music, and beautiful steps. Check out the different dance styles that Miguel, Hector, and Imelda perform in *Coco*!

Concheros

The *concheros* is a dance that includes steps from Aztec rituals. Dancers perform the steps to beating drums. They wear feather **headdresses** and colorful **loincloths**.

Colorful Ceremonies

Danza de los Voladores means "Dance of the Flyers." Indigenous people created the dance centuries ago as part of a ritual to end a severe **drought**. To perform it, five people climb a 98-foot (30 m) pole and then four of them jump. They dangle from the pole by rope tied around their ankles. The fifth person stays at the top of the pole and dances while playing a drum and a flute.

Zapateado

Zapateado is a style of dance similar to tap dancing. The dancer's steps follow along with the beat of the music. The word *zapateado* comes from the Spanish word for shoe, *zapato*. Hector and Miguel dance in this style during the performance of "Un Poco Loco."

Jarabe Tapatío

The *jarabe tapatío* is the national dance of Mexico. It is a type of *ballet folklórico*, or Mexican folk dance. The dance is typically performed by a woman and a man. The woman's costume often includes a blouse and a wide, colorful skirt. The man's costume is based on the outfit worn by charros, or traditional horsemen. The dance features precise steps, quick turns, and complicated skirt work.

CLOTHING AND FOOTWEAR

Miguel and his family come from a long line of *zapateros*, or shoemakers. The clothing worn by the extended members of the Rivera family reflect both traditional and contemporary styles. Today, fashion designers around the world find inspiration in Mexico's indigenous clothing design.

Huipil and Guayabera

The huipil is a loose-fitting blouse or dress with indigenous roots. It is usually worn by women and allows air to flow through it easily, keeping the wearer cool on a hot day. A guayabera is a shirt with buttons usually worn by men. It features two rows of carefully sewn patterns.

huipil

Sarape and Rebozo

The Mexican sarape is a woven blanket worn around the shoulders by men and women. It usually has bright and colorful designs. A rebozo is a large woven shawl or scarf that can be worn around the shoulders or the body. Sarapes and rebozos help keep the wearer shaded in the sun and warm at night. They go well with a pair of huaraches, or sandals.

sarape

China Poblana

China poblana is colorful, traditional clothing commonly worn by women in ballet folklórico. It features a white blouse and red-and-green skirt. The china poblana is a Mexican national symbol.

Charro

A charro, or a Mexican horseman, wears tough and useful clothing. Cowboy boots and a sombrero are important parts of a charro's outfit. The sombrero typically has a leather chin strap so the hat doesn't fly off while horseback riding. The modern mariachi costume has its roots in traditional charro clothing. Ernesto de la Cruz wears a white charro outfit.

ART

On his journey, Miguel meets the spirit of Frida Kahlo, a famous artist. She painted bold self-portraits with bright colors and vivid symbols. Mexico has a rich artistic history, and Mexican art continues to flourish today. Let's explore some of Mexico's artists and art forms.

Inspiring Artists

Mexico is famous for the artistry of its painters, **muralists**, and sculptors. The works of artists like Frida Kahlo, Diego Rivera, José Celemente Orozco, Maria Izquierdo, and Sebastián have inspired millions. The Palacio de Bellas Artes, or Palace of Fine Arts, in Mexico City showcases artwork by Mexican artists.

Frida Kahlo

Palacio de Bellas Artes

Artistic Traditions

Mexican folk art includes **ceramics**, weaving, leathercraft, and more. These works are unique in their use of intricate line work, vibrant colors, and fine embroidery. The region of Puebla produces a special type of painted pottery called Talavera. Tapestry artists in Oaxaca weave and embroider beautiful cloth and rugs. Shoppers in León and Guanajuato can find incredible leather goods for sale. In Jalisco and Nayarit, the Huichol people create detailed artwork with beads and yarn.

Indigenous Creativity

The indigenous people of Mexico have been creating art for thousands of years. Some examples from ancient times include cave drawings, **murals** by the Maya, and stone head sculptures by the Olmec. Aztec art featured decorated pottery, cloaks and headdresses woven from colorful feathers, and jewelry made from precious metals and stones.

Papel Picado

Using special **chisels**, Mexican artisans cut intricate designs into colorful tissue paper. Called *papel picado*, this popular art form is often seen at celebrations and fiestas. People also use *papel picado* to decorate rooms and buildings. It is a decorative feature on ofrendas during Día de Muertos.

ANCIENT STRUCTURES AND KNOWLEDGE

People in Mexico have created structures that have lasted for thousands of years. Mexican architecture includes buildings, pyramids, and cities. When Miguel visits the Land of the Dead, he sees many features that were inspired by these ancient structures. Let's explore some of them together!

Teotihuacán

Scientists continue to study the ancient ruins of Teotihuacán near Mexico City. This large city was built more than two thousand years ago. It had running water, a sewer system, living quarters, and courtyards. The Pyramid of the Sun and the Pyramid of the Moon are the largest structures in the city. They were built to line up with the sunrises and sunsets at certain times of the year. Scientists still don't know who built the city.

Chichén Itzá

The Maya people built Chichén Itzá (chee-CHEN eet-ZAH) more than one thousand years ago. The city includes a stone-lined field where the Maya played sports. The city's Pyramid of Kukulcan has broad steps. At certain times of the year, light and shadows make it appear as if the serpent god Kukulcan is climbing the steps. Miguel sees similar steps and pyramids in the Land of the Dead!

Calendars

Aztec, Olmec, and Maya people built large stone calendars to keep time by tracking the movements of the sun, planets, and stars. The Aztecs carved a calendar out of basalt, a volcanic rock. It is on display at the National Museum of Anthropology in Mexico City.

MYTHOLOGY AND FOLKLORE

In the Land of the Dead, Miguel meets a colorful winged jaguar. Pepita, Mamá Imelda's spirit guide, is a **supernatural** being inspired by Mexican myths and folktales. Mythology and **folklore** help explain what people believe about the origins of the land and people. They also explore our relationships to one another.

Founding of an Empire

Aztec myth says the god Huitzilopochtli (weet-see-loh-POHCH-tlee) claimed the people would know where to settle when they saw an eagle eating a snake while perched on a nopal cactus. After wandering for weeks, the people finally saw the eagle in a large marsh. They founded Tenochtitlán (teh-nohch-teet-LAHN), the capital of the Aztec Empire. Modern Mexico City is on this site. The eagle, snake, and cactus appear on the Mexican flag.

La Llorona

Miguel's great-great-grandmother, Imelda, sings a popular Mexican song called "La Llorona" at the Sunrise Spectacular. The song is partly inspired by the famous legend of the Weeping Woman. La Llorona is a ghost who cries as she searches for her lost children near bodies of water. Bad luck may strike anyone who crosses her path. Beware!

An Enduring Love Story

An ancient story tells how a warrior named Popocatépetl was in love with Iztaccíhuatl, a princess. He promised to marry her when he returned from battle. But a jealous rival lied to Izta, saying that Popo died in the fighting. When Popo returned, Izta had died of a broken heart. He built her a monument and stood guard over her body. Eventually, both were covered by snow and transformed into volcanoes. When smoke rises out of El Popo, it is evidence of his heart's eternal burning love.

Iztaccíhuatl

Popocatépetl

¡ADIÓS!

We've learned a lot about Miguel and his life in Mexico. His home country is full of natural beauty and wonder. We've also explored the deeply held traditions and vibrant culture of its warm, welcoming people. Mexico has a rich history and a bright, hopeful future.

Maybe one day, you'll experience
Mexico for yourself! ¡Adiós!

GLOSSARY

aqueduct: a structure that carries water, usually across long distances

architecture: the art and science of designing and building structures

astronomy: the study of things outside of Earth's atmosphere

Aztec: an indigenous population in central Mexico known for their contributions to engineering, education, astronomy, and art

Baroque period: a time of rich and showy music, art, and architecture from the seventeenth to the mid-eighteenth centuries

biome: a large region with a specific climate and particular plants and animals

ceramic: a product usually made of heated clay

chayote: a green pear-shaped vegetable with a cucumber-like flavor

chisel: a sharp hand tool used to carve or cut

civilization: an advanced human society or large group of people

climate: the average long-term weather conditions of a region

commemorate: to remember something important with a celebration or ritual

copal: dried material from tropical trees, sometimes burned as incense

corrido: a ballad in a traditional Mexican style, typically with lyrics about a historical or current event

descendant: a person related to someone from a previous generation

drought: a long period without rain

dye: a substance used to add or change the color of something

extinct: no longer existing

falsetto: a voice that is made to sound high pitched

feminine: having qualities associated with being female

folk: from or linked to the common people of a country or region

folklore: the traditional legends, stories, and beliefs of a group of people

guava: a small fruit with pink, juicy flesh and a sweet smell

habitat: the place where a plant or animal naturally lives

headdress: a ceremonial covering worn on the head

incense: a material that is burned to produce a pleasing odor

indigenous: originating naturally in a particular place

jaguar: a large wild cat that is usually yellow with black spots

jicama: a large, round root vegetable with a crisp texture and slightly sweet flavor

Latin America: the countries south of the United States where most people speak Spanish or Portuguese

livestock: farm animals

loincloth: a piece of cloth worn around the hips, usually as the only piece of clothing in a hot climate

masculine: having qualities associated with being male

Maya: an indigenous population in southern Mexico known for their contributions to architecture, astronomy, mathematics, and art

memento: an object that is kept to help remember a person, place, or event

Mexico: a large country in North America with a diverse history and population

mole: a sauce usually made with chocolate and chili peppers

mural: a large-scale painting usually done on walls

muralist: a person who paints murals

Nahuatl: a language of indigenous people in central and southern Mexico

Olmec: an ancient indigenous civilization from eastern Mexico

pan de muerto: a type of sweet bread, or pan dulce, traditionally baked for Día de Muerto

papaya: a fruit shaped like a long melon with orange flesh and small black seeds

patron saint: a religious figure that is believed to protect a person, place, or group

percussion: an instrument that is played by beating or striking it

piñata: a traditional decorated container filled with toys or candy

procession: a group of people walking as part of a ceremony

reform: a change made to improve something

resident: a person who lives in a certain place

revere: to show great respect to someone or something

ritual: a ceremony done according to social or religious custom

species: a class of plants or animals that have common attributes

supernatural: something that is beyond what humans know about the natural world

tamale: steamed cornmeal dough wrapped in a corn husk or banana leaf

tomatillo: a popular green fruit that is used in salsa verde, or green sauce

tremor: a minor earthquake

trio: a group of three musicians

urban: relating to a city

INDEX

PHOTO CREDITS